Kenneth S₂

English Missionary in Japan
1932 – 1941

Audrey Sansbury Talks

KENNETH SANSBURY

DEDICATION

For all those in Japan and elsewhere who have shown an interest in my family's life in Japan through those momentous years.

KENNETH SANSBURY

CONTENTS

Foreword

Map

1 Introduction   1

2 First Impressions   5

3 Numazu   15

4 Karuizawa   29

5 St Andrew's Church Tokyo   39

6 Shingakuin   51

7 Kofu   63

8 Chaplain to the British Embassy   71

   Afterword   81

   About the author   85

KENNETH SANSBURY

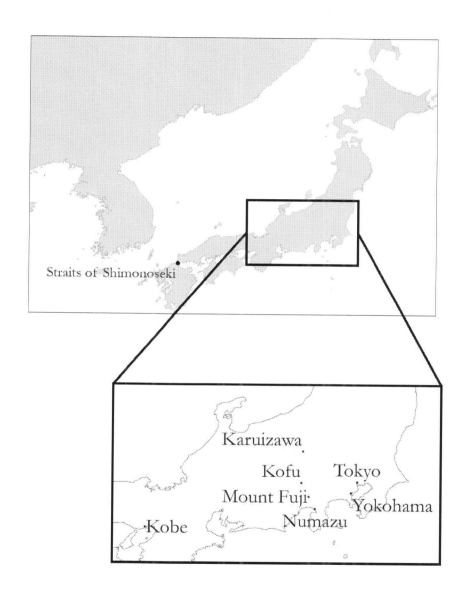

KENNETH SANSBURY

1. INTRODUCTION

Kenneth Sansbury

Kenneth Sansbury was born in London in 1905 and educated at St. Paul's School, from where he won a Scholarship to Peterhouse College, Cambridge. For his first year he studied Classics before switching to Theology, in which he gained a double First. He went on to train for the priesthood at Westcott House in Cambridge.

It was while he was still a student at Cambridge that he applied to the Society for the Propagation of the Gospel (SPG) to become a missionary in Japan. He was inspired to do this by attending a missionary rally, at which Bishop Joseph Motoda, the first Japanese Bishop of Tokyo, was one of the speakers. Bishop Motoda made clear that while the expectation was that the Nippon Sei Ko Kai (NSKK), the Anglican Church in Japan, would become independent of overseas support in due course, it was as yet a very young church and was not yet ready to stand on its own feet. He therefore appealed for missionaries to come to Japan from England and Kenneth responded to that call.

Though Kenneth had been accepted for missionary work in Japan, he could not set out until he had been ordained, first as a deacon and then as a priest, and had completed one curacy in England. He served his curacy at Dulwich Common and in 1931 he married Ethelreda Wamsley, who was a fellow student at Cambridge and whom he had met at a missionary breakfast there.

Kenneth and Ethelreda expected to sail for Japan by the end of the year, but England came off the Gold Standard in the autumn of 1931 and Bishop Matsui, Bishop Motoda's successor, sent a telegram to say that no further staff should come from England until that situation was resolved. So

Kenneth was found a temporary curacy in Wimbledon and it was not until the spring of 1932 that Kenneth and Ethelreda set sail for Yokohama.

Family group at the Port of Tilbury.
Kenneth is second from left and
Ethelreda is centre.

2. FIRST IMPRESSIONS

Kenneth Sansbury

Ethelreda Sansbury

At the end of a six weeks' voyage on the S.S. Naldera Kenneth and Ethelreda awoke to find themselves rapidly approaching the coast of Japan. They dressed quickly and went up on deck to see an impressive coastline of rugged mountains sloping down to tree-covered hills at the water's edge. The ship steamed up through the beautiful Straits of Shimonoseki to reach her anchorage between Moji on the Kyushu side and Shimonoseki on the Honshu side.

Kenneth and Ethelreda travelled on the S.S. Naldera

As they were pushing off in the launch to the shore, the Captain came hurrying down the gangway to invite them to a picnic, but when they got ashore they were met by an English lady, Miss Simeon, who said that she and another lady missionary hoped to entertain them, so they left a note for the Captain and walked up to her house.

They entered by sliding sideways a screen of lattice-work and came into a porch, where they all changed their shoes. They clambered up a steep staircase and came into an attractive sitting room with tatami mats on the floor, lattice screens covered with paper for inside walls and a verandah looking over the harbour to the hills of Kyushu. Lunch they had downstairs in western fashion, but they were greeted by the cook in Japanese fashion, bowing with her head to the floor.

After lunch and a rest Miss Simeon led them on a walk full of twists and turns to the house of the other lady missionary, Miss Kennion. On the way they called at the house of the English priest, the Rev. George Noel Strong, who served on the staff of the Bishop of Kobe from 1926 to 1928 and was priest-in-charge of Shimonoseki and Matsuyama from 1928 until the start of the Pacific War. He was away on furlough but Kenneth was impressed by what he saw: "One room is used as the local church, as in the days of the Apostles. It is beautifully arranged with a dignified altar and sanctuary and will provide a fine model for the church they soon hope to build in this place."

Miss Kennion welcomed them with tea and strawberries and showed them round the local park before guiding them back to the quayside for their launch to the ship. For Kenneth and Ethelreda this was a most interesting day, for it gave them their first insight into the life of a missionary in such a town: "It is rather lonely for some of them – in Shimonoseki there are only about half a dozen English-speaking people – and the work is not of a dramatic character: just instructing enquirers, preparing people for baptism and confirmation, looking after the children – all individual work, getting in touch with people one by one. But they seem tremendously happy in it and content to be right out of the limelight, just slogging away at laying the foundations and building up the lower parts of the walls of the Church that is gradually being raised in these places."

They sailed in the evening and for some time Kenneth and Ethelreda watched the lights on either side of the ship, but then the ship moved into a wider part of the Inland Sea and they could see nothing, so they retired and went to bed. They woke early and looked out on a most attractive scene, of green islands, both large and small, the vague line of hills marking the main island, and scores of fishing boats with their nets spread out, some propelled by a long pole and some more up-to-date with motors fitted.

They arrived in Kobe in the early afternoon and were met by an English priest, the Rev. Eric Allen, who was on the staff of the Bishop of Kobe from 1927 to 1930 and priest-in-charge of St. Peter's Kobe from 1930 until the start of the Pacific War. He brought a letter of greeting from the Bishop, who was out of Kobe for the weekend, but who gave them a very kind welcome and invited them to use his house for any meal they liked. They looked round the sights of Kobe, had tea at the chaplaincy and then went to see the church of which the Rev. Allen was in charge. Again Kenneth was impressed: "It is brand-new, beautifully light and airy, and has a most attractive altar frontal, made from a Japanese silk obi."

The next morning it was raining, so they stayed on board, but in the afternoon the ship sailed and after twenty four hours they arrived in Yokohama. They found it wonderful coming in, with the sea as smooth as a lake and the sun shining brilliantly. They were met by Bishop Heaslett, whom Kenneth described as a genial Irishman, with a great fund of humour, who made a very good companion. He took them to his house, where they met Mrs. Heaslett, who also gave them a warm welcome and made them feel very much at home. The Heasletts' house was situated on the Bluff, a long ridge running inland from a headland that protected the harbour and was the healthiest part of Yokohama for living on. The house must have been well-built, for it had survived the Great Kanto Earthquake of 1923, and what made it especially attractive was that it had views of the sea on both sides.

Bishop Samuel Heaslett had served in Japan throughout his ministry. He went out to Japan with the Church Missionary Society (CMS) in 1900, and spent the next twenty two years partly in country evangelistic work and partly in teaching in theological colleges. The only break was when he served in France with the Chinese Labour Corps during the First World War. Through those years he became fluent in the Japanese language and this fluency was an important factor in his appointment as Bishop of South Tokyo in 1922.

Bishop Heaslett invited Kenneth to accompany him to a conference of male workers in the diocese, so they caught the train to Hiratsuka, a journey of about three quarters of an hour, and went to the church where the first lecture had already begun. Kenneth knew no Japanese and so could not understand a word, but he gained a good impression of the Japanese clergy and catechists who were present. There were eighteen of them altogether; three or four were elderly or middle-aged, but for the most part they were a keen set of young men. Several of them were good scholars and the Bishop told Kenneth that some of the papers read would have been difficult for an English congregation.

Kenneth did not stay for the second paper but went for a stroll down to the shore, where he watched the fishermen pulling in their nets. It was there that he had his first view of Mount Fuji. Before it had been covered in cloud but then the cloud cleared and Fuji appeared: "It was a most glorious sight, standing out against the sky, its snow-covered slopes glistening in the sun. It is a perfect shape with its sides sloping equally up to its flat summit and I could easily see how the Japanese had come to regard it as their sacred mountain."

Mount Fuji

Kenneth returned to join the others for lunch – a real Japanese meal eaten while sitting on their heels. Fortunately he and the Bishop were provided with an extra cushion, so he was able to kneel on one and rest the other on his legs before sitting back, which made the position quite comfortable. At the end of the meal, the senior priest of the diocese gave a speech of welcome, which was translated by a young priest who had been to England. Kenneth then made a short speech in reply, which the young priest translated into Japanese. After this one of the older priests took Kenneth upstairs to see one of the treasures of the house – a sixteenth century anti-Christian notice-board, which threatened anybody who professed Christianity with death.

The following day Kenneth and Ethelreda went up to Tokyo to visit the English chaplain, the Rev. Frank Mercer, and his wife, who lived in the compound of St. Andrew's Church in Shiba. The Rev. Mercer had arrived in 1927, having had a wide experience as priest in industrial parishes in Leeds, in Western Canada and in the service of the Industrial Christian Fellowship. Kenneth later wrote of him: "He was a strong supporter of the Labour Movement and used to show his sympathy by marching in the May Day processions in Tokyo each year. His heart was in the social aspects of the Christian message, in the application of the Gospel to the economic and industrial life of the world, in the better ordering of society, so that the evils he had seen at close quarters in Leeds and elsewhere might be done away." Now his time as chaplain was coming to a close and he and his wife were returning to England, so Bishop Heaslett hoped that Kenneth could help to fill the gap.

That evening the Bishop talked with Kenneth about his plans for their future. The Bishop's idea was that they should spend two years in Numazu, a small coastal town in the north-west corner of the Izu Peninsula, where they would study the language with a tutor. A missionary, Miss Edlin, was returning to England and so her house would become available. It was now the beginning of June and in the middle of July they would go to the famous holiday resort of Karuizawa for six weeks and their tutor would accompany them. At the beginning of September they would return to Numazu and every other weekend they would go up to Tokyo, where Kenneth would take services at the English Church in Shiba. After two years they would move to Tokyo where Kenneth would join the staff of the Shingakuin (Central Theological College) in Ikebukuro. But first they must learn the language.

FIRST IMPRESSIONS

3. NUMAZU

St John's Church, Numazu

They travelled to Numazu by train – a three hour journey by slowish train from Yokohama. They passed at first through a landscape of small tree-covered hills and of barley and rice fields and fruit trees on the flat part of the ground. After a while the train climbed up to a pass not very far from Mount Fuji, then wound its way through a deep ravine, crossing from one side to the other and often going through tunnels. The scenery was glorious, with steep slopes on each side, waterfalls here and there, and a stream running through the bottom of the valley. They then descended to flatter scenery, catching a momentary glimpse of Mount Fuji on the way, and arrived safely in Numazu.

Mount Fuji from Numazu Bay

There they were welcomed by Miss Edlin, the missionary whose house they would be moving into. They were eager to see their new home and when they had explored it they were delighted. It was a compact and comfortable Japanese house, built of wood, with tatami mats on the floors, plenty of air and light through the open verandahs and a view of Mount Fuji from their beds. They were glad too that Miss Edlin would be with them for their first six weeks, for she was good company and would be invaluable in helping Ethelreda to understand Japanese housekeeping.

Kenneth and Ethelreda's house in Numazu

This was the start of the rainy season and so for the first few days they stayed at home and settled in, but by Sunday the rain had cleared and they walked to church in sunshine. St. John's Church was quite large for a Japanese country church and was built in a fairly modern style that harmonised well with the surrounding houses. Bishop Heaslett had spoken to Kenneth about the members of staff. Moriyasu-san, the priest-in-charge, was a fine preacher and scholar, who liked to spend time in studying books of theology. Masamichi Imai, the catechist, was very clever and had a strong

18

missionary spirit, working hard to build up the church and increase its membership in Numazu and the country around. Minnamioka-san, the woman worker, had spent time at St. Christopher's College at Blackheath in London and so knew all about Sunday School work, as well as being capable at most other things too.

The services varied according to the Sunday in the month. On the first and third Sundays there was a pre-Communion service (a shortened form of Matins and Litany) and a Sung Celebration at 10 a.m., while on the other Sundays there was Holy Communion at 7 a.m. and Matins and Sermon at 10 a.m. In the summer the evening service was always at 7.30 p.m.

This being the first Sunday in June, therefore, there was pre-Communion and a Sung Celebration, and a very interesting experience it was for Kenneth and Ethelreda to hear everything in Japanese for the first time. They were given prayer books in romaji (Japanese written in Roman script) and so were able to follow everything pretty clearly, but the hymns were beyond them, for the hymn books were in Japanese script. Afterwards the congregation went through to the church room, a fine Japanese room next door to the church, where they all sat on the floor and drank Japanese tea. Here Kenneth and Ethelreda were as friendly and sociable as they could be when all they could say in Japanese was 'Good morning', 'Thank you' and 'Good-bye'!

The next day they began language lessons with their tutor, Yorimichi Imai. He was the brother of the catechist, Masamichi Imai, and they were sons of the former Principal of the Shingakuin in Tokyo. That week Kenneth and Ethelreda spent trying to learn the Japanese characters.

Kenneth found this difficult: "With her quick memory, Ethelreda is very good at them, while with my poor memory I am very bad. There are about fifty sounds in Japanese and each sound has two characters to represent it – what are called katakana and hiragana. This means that we have to master one hundred Japanese characters. Only when we have done that do we begin to learn the far more difficult Chinese characters, so you can see we have a pretty stiff task ahead of us!"

Language lessons in Numazu

The next weekend was an eventful one in Numazu. Bishop Heaslett arrived on Saturday afternoon for a Confirmation on Sunday morning, when seven candidates were presented. After the service the congregation adjourned to the church room, where Moriyasu San gave a speech of welcome to the Bishop and to Kenneth and Ethelreda. They then all had a picnic lunch together. Apparently this was a very popular custom in the churches, and nearly every one had this common meal on one Sunday in the month. Kenneth thought it "an excellent idea and definitely primitive Christianity".

But the weather in Numazu was becoming increasingly warm and sultry, so that every effort was exhausting. As the heat was very damp, possessions began to be covered in mildew and this damp heat brought out the insects and especially the mosquitoes. Then the rains came and on one day combined with a mild typhoon. The wind blew furiously, whirling the rain round in great gusts and eddies, so the shutters on the south side of the house had to be closed and the house became filled with a steamy heat. It was a relief when the day came to leave for Karuizawa.

It was mid-September by the time they returned to Numazu and Kenneth was greeted with a message that gave him a shock. Moriyasu-san was to be absent the following Sunday at an out-station and so Kenneth was to celebrate Holy Communion in Japanese. Nor was he to be initiated gradually at a quiet service with just a few communicants. It was the third Sunday in the month and therefore the service was the main one of the day with the full morning congregation present. For the rest of the week Yorimichi-san practised diligently with Kenneth, first at home and then in church, where Kenneth stood at the altar and he at the back of the church. Kenneth thought the result was not too bad for a first effort, though with a good many stumbles and plenty of mispronunciations. Yorimichi-san was pleased, however, and wrote to Bishop Heaslett: "Mr. Moriyasu was absent Sunday and asked Communion to Mr. Sansbury. I was rather worried but it is only anxiousness. He had wonderful success. There was no mistake, and very nice tone and accent. If one had heard his voice from outside the door one would have thought it was a Japanese priest holding the service. He came only three months ago to Japan. Isn't it a record?"

The following month Kenneth and Ethelreda were due to entertain the members of the church for a meeting, partly religious and partly social. It was the custom on Wednesday evenings for members of the congregation to meet in each other's houses, where the host would announce the hymns, lead in prayer and deliver a brief address. So on the day of the visit Yorimichi-san came to the house and he and Kenneth decided what should be done. First Kenneth would make a short speech in Japanese, apologising for his ignorance of the language and welcoming them as members of the church to their home. Then he would announce a hymn and say two or three prayers from the Japanese Prayer Book. After that he would read a short address in English and Moriyasu-san would translate it into Japanese.

About twenty people arrived for the meeting and Kenneth felt it passed off well, though he was not sure how many of his Japanese remarks could be understood. After him two or three people made short speeches and after a second hymn about the same number joined in prayer. Moriyasu-san closed with the Blessing. Then came the social part of the evening when tea was served and each person was given cakes and biscuits on a piece of white paper to eat there or take home. Yorimichi-san later told Kenneth that almost all the prayers had been for them, asking for special protection for them, because they were so far from their native land.

Kenneth also began to hold a weekly Bible class in English, mainly for teachers from several schools in Numazu. For the first class, on St. Luke's Gospel, he wrote out all he intended to say, in order to be sure his words were simple, and Masamichi-san cyclostyled the various points in English and in Japanese Kenneth also showed pictures from the 'Encyclopaedia Britannica' and other books and they seemed very interested. One member of the group was a rhododendron grower, who belonged to the 'Gospel Church', so he already knew something of Christianity. Another was a bus driver, who came with his bus and parked it outside the house.

Kenneth also began to read a book of pastoral theology with Masamichi-san. The idea was that they should read this book together, so that they could discuss its contents and so that Masamichi-san might improve his English and Kenneth might improve his Japanese. Kenneth was glad to have these various commitments, as he wanted to contribute to the life of the church in Numazu, but was limited by his lack of Japanese. As he said: "It is going to be a long time before one is any real use in this land of involved sentences and complicated thought forms."

The time came for Kenneth and Ethelreda to take their first exams in Japanese. The written papers were sent from Tokyo and proved easier than they expected, for they did not cover nearly all the material supplied by the language school. Then came the oral exam and again this proved easier than they expected, for they did not have to hold a conversation in Japanese, but were instead asked to say sentences bringing in various words and phrases.

Kenneth and Ethelreda were spending Christmas in Tokyo, as Kenneth was taking the services for the English congregation of St. Andrew's Church in Shiba. But before they left for Tokyo there were preparations in Numazu. The church kindergarten gave a Christmas party and display. The kindergarten room was most attractively decorated with a Christmas tree as its crowning feature. After the party there was a final dress rehearsal for the tableaux on Christmas night. Kenneth had chosen seven scenes — the Annunciation, the visit to Elizabeth, the Nativity, the vision of the shepherds, the worship by the shepherds, the appearance of the star to the wise men and the worship of the wise men. The last scene made a good climax: at the back of the stage four angels stood in a row; in the centre was Mary, with Joseph standing beside her; the three shepherds were kneeling on the right side of the stage, while at the left the three wise men were in single file, the front one kneeling and the other two standing. While this tableau was being shown, the hymn 'O come, all ye faithful' was sung and at the end of the first verse two children in full Japanese dress entered from the right and knelt before Mary.

In the New Year came a change at the church. Yorimichi Imai was now ready to be appointed as a full-time catechist in the diocese and Bishop Heaslett had decided that he should become catechist in Numazu, while his brother Masamichi Imai should move on from Numazu to become catechist in Shizuoka. The people were very upset by the departure of Masamichi-san. At the next house meeting many people expressed their sorrow at his leaving and on the day of his departure many people came to the station to bid him a respectful farewell.

Kenneth now began to teach in the Commercial School. He was rather nervous about this at first, as he had little idea of how much English the boys would know, but he found it not too challenging, as he was only required to hear the boys read and explain very simply any difficulties in the story. He found the boys could read quite fast, but could understand nothing of what he said! This was because they had been taught to read quite difficult books, but little attention had been given to oral training. So if they saw the word DOG written in a book, they would know what it meant, but they would have no idea what it meant if they heard an English person pronounce it!

Kenneth was to take a service in Shimizu, a town with a fine harbour on the west side of Suruga Bay. The church was situated not in the centre but on the outskirts of the town and a series of removals meant that the congregation had been sadly depleted, so that when the deacon-in-charge had arrived in the previous April he found that all the keenest people had gone and only the less keen were left. Kenneth celebrated in the little room-church before a congregation of just eight people, but the deacon was a good worker and was gradually making fresh contacts. This was shown at the end of the Celebration when Kenneth baptised the father of a family whose son acted as his godfather!

Kenneth and Ethelreda took another exam, which was distinctly harder than the first one. In addition to the oral part, which was quite short, they had two long written papers which took over two hours each. The position was not made easier by the fact that one paper was based on a book they had not received from the language school, so while they had studied a book that would form part of the course in the future, they were sent a paper based on a book which had formed part of the course in the past. Kenneth wrote a stern letter to the language school and hoped the matter would soon be put right!

Kenneth went again to Shimizu and found that the congregation, which had been so depleted by people moving away, had begun to build up again. There were now twelve keen new members and Kenneth baptised three of them at the service, a husband and wife and another woman. In addition to their Japanese names the married couple took the names of Aquila and Priscilla, the members of the tent-making fraternity who became companions of St. Paul.

Kenneth and Ethelreda were invited to supper at the home of Minnamioka-san, the woman worker, and her elderly mother. They were given a delicious Japanese meal and felt encouraged that they were able to hold a conversation in Japanese for two whole hours, though the conversation was kept at a fairly simple level or they knew they would have got into difficulties.

The deacon-in-charge from Shimizu, Hayashi-san, came to stay, so that Kenneth could supervise him as he sat the exams to become a priest. He stayed for three days and on each day took three two hour exams, so nine exams in all. Kenneth was pleased to have this opportunity to become better acquainted with him and found him a most interesting person. Many of the Japanese clergy were at least second generation Christians, but Hayashi-san had been brought up as a Buddhist. He studied science and had the opportunity of joining his brother in a flourishing engineering business

Kenneth and Ethelreda spent their first summers in Japan in the mountain resort of Karuizawa. This resort was founded by Archdeacon Alexander Croft Shaw (1848-1902), an influential SPG missionary, born and educated in Canada, who arrived in Japan in 1873. In the summer of 1886 he was travelling with his family through the hills, looking for a cool place to stay. On 8 August they arrived in Karuizawa, liked it and stayed for the rest of the summer. Others followed their example and Karuizawa's popularity as a mountain resort was established.

By 1932 many missionaries regularly spent their summers in Karuizawa. Some had houses of their own, while others rented accommodation. Kenneth and Ethelreda had arrived in Japan too late to rent a house for their first summer, so they boarded with Miss Tristram, the daughter of the late Canon Tristram of Durham. She had served in Japan as a CMS missionary for more than forty years, having been headmistress of the Poole Girls' School in Osaka. She had now retired and been succeeded by a Japanese headmistress. She received a pension and could have returned to England, but felt she could be of help to old girls of the school and devoted most of her time to them. The rest of her time she gave to the Garden Home, a preventative place for those with a tendency to consumption. During the holiday she organised a sale of work in a shop in the main village street in Karuizawa to raise funds for the Garden Home and also for the Leper Settlement at Kusatsu, which was about a three hour journey away by train. She was over seventy but was full of activity and bustled about like someone many years younger.

Main street in Karuizawa

The summer chaplain in Karuizawa was the Rev. James Chappell, an Englishman who had taught in the middle and high schools in Gifu and been instrumental in setting up the Gifu School for the Blind. He had been taking the summer services at Christ Church, Karuizawa for thirty-four years or so. The services were held in English, as in the summer there was a large English-speaking population. They consisted of Holy Communion at 8 a.m., Morning Prayer and Sermon at 10.30 a.m. and Evensong and Intercessions at 5.30 p.m. Kenneth found the services somewhat old-fashioned, but Mr. Chappell explained that he was cautious in the mornings, as many of the older missionaries had last attended services regularly in England in the 1890s, and might be dismayed by anything too modern.

Soon after their arrival Kenneth preached at Christ Church one Sunday before a congregation that included three bishops. He found this somewhat daunting, but reflected that it could have been four or five, for there were quite a number of senior clergy among the missionaries staying in Karuizawa. There was Bishop McKim, the veteran American Bishop of North Tokyo, who was staying with Mr. Chappell. He was eighty years old and somewhat deaf, but apart from that he was active and alert and still going strong. There was Bishop Hamilton, who was Bishop of mid-Japan, the diocese supported by the Canadian Church, who was there with his wife and daughter. He had been in Japan for forty years and would be retiring in the following year. And then there was Bishop Heaslett, who had a house high on the hillside overlooking Karuizawa, and was spending the summer there with his wife.

Kenneth and Ethelreda soon established a pattern for their stay. The mornings were mostly spent in language study, for their tutor had also come to Karuizawa and with so many English speakers around they needed to keep working at their Japanese. Afternoons were spent in resting, reading and writing and then after tea they would go for walks. Evenings were spent in reading, chatting or going out. Sunday, of course, was different and Monday was a free day, so then they could go on the longer walks for which Karuizawa was famous.

On one such walk Kenneth and Ethelreda set out with four companions. Bishop Heaslett arrived dressed for a major expedition, in a large khaki sun helmet, an open-neck khaki shirt, fawn-coloured riding breeches, puttees and hefty studded walking boots. The other three were all from Kyushu. The Rev. James Hind was a CMS missionary. He was now over 70 and retired, but still chose to remain in Japan. Two or three years earlier he had had an illness which stopped his walking expeditions for a time, but he was now quite fit again and strode across the country as strongly as any of the others. Canon Archibald Hutchinson, who came with his wife, was also a CMS missionary. Kenneth described him as having a dry sense of humour and a wide range of interests, while she was unreservedly cheerful and could be relied upon to dress well – "no mean accomplishment in this place of pre-war styles".

Hiking expedition

Canon Hutchinson belonged to a family with deep roots in Japan. His father, Archdeacon Arthur Hutchinson, had come to Japan from Hong Kong in 1882 and served in Kyushu diocese, being based first in Nagasaki and then in Fukuoka, before returning to Nagasaki as archdeacon in 1911. He died in Karuizawa in 1918 and was buried there. His son Archibald had been born in Nagasaki in 1889 and returned to Japan in 1909. He was now Canon in Fukuoka.

His younger brother, Ernest, had come out to Japan in 1916 and was now serving in the Kansai.

A committee meeting of the church was held at the house of Mr. and Mrs. Waller, another family with deep roots in Japan, for they had served there with the Canadian Mission for very many years. Kenneth said of Mr. Waller that he probably knew more of Karuizawa than any other living man and was a very good businessman, as well as a very nice person, while his wife was short and stout and poured forth good nature and motherliness on all around. They had two sons, one ordained and also working in the Canadian diocese and one working in the Hong Kong and Shanghai Bank in Kobe.

An afternoon tea party was held at the next door house, which belonged to two ladies, Miss Boyd and Miss Mander, who taught at a school in Tokyo and who did a good deal of missionary work on their own for the NSKK, although not attached to any society. They were very good company, kept themselves up-to-date with new books and had everything in the house very tastefully arranged. They were ladies with private means and provided a splendid tea for missionaries of the NSKK spending the summer in Karuizawa.

Another of the many single lady missionaries staying in Karuizawa was Miss Marie Bath, who had come to Japan the previous year to be secretary to Miss Hannah Riddell. When Miss Riddell first arrived in Japan in 1895 she had been horrified by the condition of lepers in Kumamoto in Kyushu and found her vocation in establishing and running a hospital for their care. She had died in the spring of 1932 and Miss Bath would move on to the leper hospital founded by Miss Cornwall Legh in Kusatsu. There she would seek to provide employment for the healthy children of lepers, so that they could become self-supporting, for they were not accepted in society.

There were many Americans staying in Karuizawa and Kenneth and Ethelreda were invited to lunch at the home of Bishop Nickolls and his wife and their four delightful children. Bishop Heaslett was also a guest, as were two lady missionaries, one American and the other English. The English lady, Miss Philips, told how she once missed her train connection and could not catch another train until about one in the morning. She was feeling very tired, when an industrious Japanese student started to cross-question her about everything in England and finally, to her great embarrassment, persuaded her to sing 'It's a long way to Tipperary' in front of all the passengers in the carriage!

Kenneth and Ethelreda also had acquaintances among the Japanese staying in Karuizawa and were invited to a tea party at the house of the Sekiya family. Mr. Sekiya was Vice-Chamberlain of the Imperial Household and so he was away in Tokyo but Mrs. Sekiya was staying there with three of their sons and three daughters. It was in fact the eldest son, Paul, whom Kenneth and Ethelreda already knew, for he was studying at Westcott House, a theological college in Cambridge, and had stayed with them several times in Wimbledon. He would be returning to Japan at the end of the year and was to be ordained in the NSKK in the following year.

One of Paul's brothers had just begun to study philosophy at the Imperial University in Tokyo and he began to call round on Sunday afternoons to discuss with Kenneth matters relating to religion and philosophy. One afternoon they had been talking for about an hour and a quarter when he asked Kenneth to give his impressions of the effect of Christianity on Japanese life as compared with the effect of Christianity on English life. Kenneth was relieved that tea arrived just at that moment, so he could postpone answering such a huge question till the following week. But he found it very interesting to have these discussions and to learn something of the way Japanese students were thinking.

Kenneth and Ethelreda were also invited to the house of the Watanabe family in Kutenkake, the next village to Karuizawa. Viscount Watanabe, like Mr. Sekiya, was kept in Tokyo by official duties, but Viscountess Watanabe and her two sons gave them a very warm welcome. One son had been a paying guest at the Vicarage in Wimbledon and while there had visited them often. Now he had returned to Japan via the United States and over tea he showed them some of the 1500 photos he had taken during his fourteen months abroad! He had a small German camera which took tiny prints, but took them so well that they enlarged excellently to postcard size.

Early in September it was time to return to Numazu, for the season was coming to an end in Karuizawa, summer residents were returning to their places of work and soon the place would be almost empty. Kenneth and Ethelreda felt very grateful for the time they had spent in Karuizawa, for they had made many new friends, learnt about the life of the Church in different parts of Japan and felt that wherever they went in Japan they would be sure to find someone they knew.

KARUIZAWA

5. ST. ANDREW'S CHURCH, TOKYO

St. Andrew's Church, Tokyo (English congregation)

In September 1932 Kenneth began his chaplaincy duties for the English congregation at St. Andrew's Church in Shiba, so on two Sundays each month he would go up by train to Tokyo from Numazu and on the other two Sundays other clergy from Tokyo or Yokohama would take the services there. On the first occasion, he celebrated at the 8 a.m. service and preached at 11 a.m. Many Tokyo people were not yet back from their holidays and so it was doubtful if there would be any congregation but a few turned up at 8 a.m. and nearly twenty five at 11 a.m., including the Ambassador, who read the first lesson. As the rain was pouring down just before the service and forty was considered a good number at the best of times, this seemed an encouraging start.

After the service Kenneth and Ethelreda were invited to a lunch party at the home of Mr. Carey, the secretary of the Church Committee, and his wife, and had a most enjoyable time. But when Kenneth next took the services at St. Andrew's, Mr. Carey told him that later that day they had suffered a sad catastrophe, for in the evening their house was gutted by fire and they lost all their possessions.

Early in November Kenneth was to preach at the Armistice Day service, which was always held in St. Andrew's on the Sunday before Armistice Day. Kenneth knew this was an important event in the life of the British community in Tokyo and so he wrote out his sermon in full, both to give more dignity to his delivery and to avoid any pitfalls in speaking on the somewhat delicate subject of peace. For the service there was a grand attendance: the British Ambassador and the Canadian Minister, who read the lessons, all the Embassy and Legation officials, including the Army, Navy and Air Force attaches, and a large section of

British Tokyo residents.

After the service Kenneth and Ethelreda were invited to the home of Mr. and Mrs. Lewis for pre-lunch drinks. Mr. Lewis was organist at the church and also chairman of the Tokyo branch of the British Legion and so it was his custom on Armistice Day to invite British Legion members and others back to their home. Afterwards they went on to the home of Mr. and Mrs. McKenlay. Mr. McKenlay, who was choirmaster at the church, worked as adviser to the Mitsubishi Fire and Marine Insurance Company and in his spare time arranged most of the musical activities among the foreign community in Tokyo. The other guests at the lunch were Captain Kennedy and his wife. Captain Kennedy was an ex-language officer, who had lost a leg in the War and so was invalided out of the army. He was now Reuters correspondent in Tokyo and Kenneth described him as a most charming and interesting man.

In the afternoon Kenneth and Ethelreda were invited to tea at the Canadian Legation by the Minister's wife, Mrs. Marler, who was Chairman of the St. Andrew's Ladies' Guild. She was most hospitable and went out of her way to be kind to them, for she put a Legation car at their disposal for the following morning, invited them to stay a night the following week, when a special meeting of the Guild was taking place, and even invited them to stay at the Legation for Christmas.

The next special services at St. Andrew's were for Harvest Thanksgiving Day in November. This was certainly later than harvest festivals in England, which would take place in October. This difference was due to there being two harvests in Japan, a wheat and barley harvest at the end of May and beginning of June and a rice harvest in November.

The English time therefore would be too late for the first harvest and too early for the second. As it was, the services went well: there were good congregations for both and the church was pleasingly decorated with fruit and flowers.

The following day Kenneth and Ethelreda visited the house where four Sisters of the Community of the Epiphany of Truro lived. The Community had been associated with Japan for a long time and Kenneth described them as "a great power for good in the Sei Ko Kai". They had an orphanage and an embroidery school and also provided retreats and quiet times both for women missionaries and for Japanese women workers.

In the same compound as the Sisters' House was the SPG High School for Girls, the Koran Jo Gakko, and the houses for the three foreign teachers, Miss Tanner, Miss Wooley and Miss Hailstone. The school was in a lovely position on a small eminence with beautiful gardens round and a view of Mount Fuji, sixty miles away, in the distance.

On Christmas Eve Kenneth and Ethelreda caught a train about noon from Numazu to Tokyo and, after some shopping in the Ginza, went on to the Canadian Legation. There dinner was followed by carols sung by the Tokyo Madrigal Club and by the opening of presents. Later they set off for the midnight Choral Celebration at the American church, Holy Trinity. This was a fine service with a very large congregation and with the church most attractively decorated and lit by candles only.

On Christmas Day itself Kenneth took the 8 a.m. Holy Communion and then the 11 a.m. Choral Celebration at St. Andrew's and later the 5.30 p.m. Evensong, which was held mainly for the benefit of missionaries who would have attended Japanese services in the morning. Then Kenneth and Ethelreda returned to the Legation, where twenty-eight sat down for Christmas dinner. The guests included the Apostolic Delegate, whom Kenneth described as "a cheery, broadminded Irish American", Dr. Mackenzie, the senior missionary from Canada and a Methodist, the Legation staff and their wives, two girls who were spending the winter at the Legation and Kenneth and Ethelreda. After a traditional Christmas dinner, with turkey sent from Canada, the ladies withdrew to the morning room, while the men adjourned to the library for coffee, until they were all called back into the drawing room to watch a silent Buster Keaton film which had not yet been released in Japan.

In February planning began for services for Lent and Easter at the two English-speaking churches in Tokyo, St. Andrew's and Holy Trinity, for although each church had its own clergy, its own congregation and its own choir, yet at certain times of year they planned their programme together. In fact, from time to time meetings were held to discuss the possibility of the two congregations merging, but the difficulty always arose that each was happy to combine, as long as the united services continued in their own church building.

On Good Friday there was a 10 a.m. service at St. Andrew's, but Kenneth did not attend, as he was taking the Three Hours' Service at Holy Trinity. He felt this went well and was surprised by the number of people who came and by the number who stayed throughout. For Holy Week observances were not easy in Japan, where businesses carried on as usual and where schools had already begun the summer term if Easter came late.

Easter Day too passed off well. Kenneth celebrated at St. Andrew's at 8 a.m., when there was a good congregation, and then exchanged with the American, Bishop Reifsnider, to celebrate at Holy Trinity at 11 a.m., when the veteran Bishop McKim was preaching.

Kenneth found these connections with the English-speaking churches very rewarding, for the parishioners were mainly professional people and many had lived and worked in different countries and so had a broad experience through their travels. And, of course, it was satisfying for him to have this English language work while he was not yet proficient in the Japanese language.

In June the number of people attending services began to decline, as people left the heat of Tokyo to go on holiday. Many of the business families went to places on the coast, such as Hayama and Kamakura, where they had the sea air to cool them, and from where they could travel up to Tokyo for business quite easily, as a frequent electric train service took only fifty minutes. Several of these families would be away from Tokyo for about three months, so Kenneth suggested to Bishop Heaslett the idea of holding a service along that piece of coast once or twice during the summer. Some people were rather doubtful about the plan, but at the first such service fourteen foreigners and nine Japanese attended, so it was felt to be well worthwhile and the Celebration was certainly appreciated by those who were present.

In October the Secretary of SPG, Canon Waddy, visited Japan. This was the time when the Tokyo Diocesan Synod was taking place and Canon Waddy addressed a morning session. He was an Australian by birth and Kenneth wrote that his hearty manner, cheerful appearance and obvious friendliness won over his listeners very quickly. In the afternoon the clergy of the diocese presented him with a gift as a mark of gratitude for his visit and for the help of SPG over many years. The senior priest in the diocese made a speech, which was also read in translation by one of the younger men. Kenneth described this as a most moving document, expressing great gratitude for all the SPG had meant to them and describing how much had been done by SPG men and their teaching. Kenneth hoped Canon Waddy would get this address printed in one of the SPG papers, as he felt it would be a great encouragement to people in England who were supporting their mission.

In the spring of 1934 Kenneth and Ethelreda and their baby son Christopher moved to Tokyo for, after two years of language study, Kenneth was ready to take up his role as a lecturer at the Shingakuin (the Central Theological College) which was attached to Rikkyo (St. Paul's University) in Ikebukuro. This was to be his principal occupation, but his second occupation was as Chaplain to the British community, for now that he was living in Tokyo, the temporary arrangement by which he had travelled up to Tokyo from Numazu twice a month to take services came to an end and he became officially Chaplain to the British community.

Once again the Easter services at St. Andrew's went well, in spite of pouring rain. The church was most attractively decorated with lilies and cherry blossom and there was a good congregation, including the Duchess of Northumberland and her two daughters who were making a round the world cruise. After the service Kenneth made a

Soon after arriving in Numazu Kenneth had an opportunity to meet some of the students from the Shingakuin, the theological college in Ikebukuro. They were holding a mission in Shimizu, where the congregation of the church had been depleted by a series of removals, and were hoping through this mission to bring in new enquirers. The mission was held over a weekend and Kenneth travelled with Dr. Shaw, a lecturer at the Shingakuin, to join the students for the final evening and then to celebrate for them on the following day.

Kenneth was impressed by the effort the students made. Before the mission they painted a large number of posters which they stuck all over the town. For about an hour before the meeting they went round the town with home-made cardboard megaphones announcing the meeting and handing out handbills to all passers-by. The meeting began about 7.45 p.m. and consisted of an informal service with an address, which lasted about an hour and a quarter. On the two nights of the mission they got into touch with about forty new people in addition to those who attended their open-air talks in the middle of the day. As Kenneth said, this seemed small by what one might expect in England, but then numbers in Japan were small and there was no likelihood of rapid expansion in the near future. The day after the mission the students were given a day out after all their hard work and were taken to two hot springs on the Izu peninsula – an outing everyone enjoyed.

After the mission and the visit to the hot springs Kenneth set off with Dr. Shaw for Ikebukuro, where a reunion of former students was taking place at the Shingakuin. This visit was of special interest to Kenneth, as it was likely that he and Ethelreda would be moving to the Shingakuin themselves after two years of language study and acclimatisation in Numazu.

They passed the entrance to Rikkyo (St. Paul's University), which was almost opposite the theological college and which was built of brick in western style. They then came to the theological college where the buildings were of wood and where there were attractive grounds with plenty of trees and an open field for playing games. As they approached from the road, they passed two houses for western staff and a tennis court on the right and the playing field on their left. At the far end stood the three main college buildings: on the right the building containing the lecture rooms, hall, etc.; in the centre the chapel; and on the left the students' dormitory and common room. Four houses for Japanese staff stood to the left of the playing field.

Rikkyo (St Paul's University), Ikebukuro, Tokyo

The three western members of staff with their
families: (from left to right) back row: Kenneth
(holding Helen), Stanley Woodward, Larry
Rose; centre row: Ethelreda, Gwen Woodward
(holding John), Caroline Rose;
front row: Christopher, Peggy Rose, David
Woodward, Audrey, Peter Woodward

Celebration and visiting. Later they hoped that Masamichi-san would be sent to live in Kofu and begin work there.

After the meeting Kenneth and Miss Shepherd went to the Canadian Methodist school, where she had been staying, and after drinking tea they made the two hour bus journey through the mountains to Yoshida, where they visited another solitary Christian. She was not in very good circumstances, but was very keen and usually when Miss Shepherd visited she gathered her friends and neighbours together so that Miss Shepherd could hold a meeting. This time, however, she had not been well and so had not been able to do this. On the following morning, Kenneth celebrated for her, the first time she had received Communion in thirteen years. Here again she showed her keenness, for as she had been unwell Kenneth and Miss Shepherd planned to hold the Celebration at her house, but she did not want to give them the trouble of a rather long walk and so she set out at 5 a.m. to find the inn where they were staying, so the Celebration could be held there, even though she was by no means fit after her illness.

Kenneth had come to know Masamichi-san well during the time that he was catechist in Numazu and so in October 1933 Kenneth went to Yokohama for his Ordination as a priest. Kenneth described it as a very impressive service with some twenty robed clergy, including Canon Waddy, being present. He said the church had been built after the 1923 earthquake in admirable style and made an excellent setting for such ceremonies. He thought Masamichi-san found the service very inspiring.

Kenneth then made his second visit to Kofu. This time there were four communicants and as one who had come the previous time could not be there, this meant there were two new people. This was encouraging and although he recognised that it would be uphill work for some time, he felt that with regular services and visits a church would be established there.

Kenneth was pleased with his November visit to Kofu, when he delivered his sermon in Japanese, which meant that he read it from manuscript. The people who heard it showed their customary Japanese politeness, but he was quite pleased himself and felt he had read it not too badly for a first attempt. It had been a great deal of work to prepare and he thought he must have spent twelve to sixteen hours writing and correcting and revising it, but he felt it had been worth the time and effort taken and that it was one of the best ways in which he could make progress with his Japanese.

In December Kenneth was in Tokyo for a meeting and afterwards took the train to Kofu, arriving about 11.30 p.m. He had left Tokyo in rain, but Kofu was a good deal higher than Tokyo and as the train climbed, the rain turned to snow. When he left the station he found about four inches of snow on the ground and was not sorry to have a hot bath and get into bed at the inn. The following morning they had their service, but only the two most faithful ventured through the snow. This time he gave a shortened version of the first sermon he had preached in Numazu and after the service they drank tea and chatted until lunch time. He caught the afternoon train back to Numazu and found there had been no snow there, only heavy rain and wind.

In January 1934 Kenneth wrote that Masamichi-san was being sent to Kofu to live there as a resident deacon, while he would continue to go once a month for Celebrations and to keep an eye on how things were going. As he said, this was an advance on any previous plan and meant the beginning of something definite there.

On Kenneth's February visit to Kofu, therefore, he and Masamichi-san spent the Saturday afternoon looking for a suitable house in the district to the north of the station. They decided on this district because there was no other church on that side of the railway line at all and the district was a growing one with many new houses being built. By good fortune the very first house they went to see proved just right. It was a two-storied house with five rooms to the left of the porch and a foreign-style room built on to the right of the porch. That room was panelled all round and would make a splendid chapel, quite big enough for present purposes. So they felt very elated. It seemed they were led at once to the right house, which was so suitable that it might have been built for them. They ordered a table for an altar and some chairs and hoped by the next month to be sufficiently ready for services.

And indeed in March they did hold their first service there. There were only three people there beside themselves, but Masamichi-san, who was now living there, was very keen and was hoping to start a Sunday School almost at once for the neighbouring children, so there was the prospect of development. Meanwhile Kenneth donated the salary that he received from his teaching at the Commercial School in Numazu to encourage this work in Kofu.

In April Kenneth attended the wedding of Masamichi-san. He described it as a grand occasion with a fully choral service and a Nuptial Mass, at which he celebrated. He described this as a nerve-racking ordeal before experienced missionaries and rows of Japanese clergy. He thought Masamichi-san's bride seemed a very nice girl who would be a great help to him in his work. After the wedding, in accordance with Japanese custom, they were making a round of visits to the bridegroom's relatives before settling into their new home in Kofu.

It was just after this that Kenneth and Ethelreda moved to Ikebukuro, but Kenneth continued to make the monthly journey to Kofu, which took three and a half hours, until the time of their return to England on furlough in July 1937. By that time it was becoming difficult for foreigners to work among Japanese people and so when they returned to Japan in 1938 Kenneth no longer travelled to Kofu. He and Masamichi-san remained good friends, however, and Kenneth was godfather to Masamichi-san's eldest son, Isaac.

And so Kenneth and Ethelreda and their family returned to Japan in the summer of 1938 sailing on the Hikawa Maru with the protection provided by their new diplomatic passports. Kenneth would combine his work as chaplain to the British Embassy with his work as chaplain to the English church of St. Andrew's in Shiba, so his English chaplaincy work would become his principal role. His work as lecturer at the Shingakuin could continue, though in a more limited way, while his oversight of the Japanese church in Kofu would cease altogether.

At Jiyu Gakuen (kindergarten in Tokyo) Audrey at back, Christopher in front of her, David Woodward towards right

This shrinking of Kenneth's work among the Japanese was symptomatic of a general trend among missionaries in Japan to find doors closing against them, but Kenneth felt that his chaplaincy work was more than ever appreciated by an increasingly anxious and unsettled British community. He said of St. Andrew's in Shiba that the restitution of an Embassy chaplain in a paid capacity, which made possible a more or less full-time man for English work in Tokyo, had given the church a new lease of life: "The people feel they have their own chaplain again and the psychological effect of that is good." Despite a tendency for the British community to grow smaller, the congregations were remaining level at about fifty on a Sunday morning as an average through the year. Kenneth was disappointed, however, in the number of communicants attending the 8 a.m. service. There were only about fifty on Christmas Day and only about five to seven on an average Sunday morning. This was partly due to distances. Tokyo was a large city and the foreign community lived scattered all over the various districts and was not concentrated in one or two areas, as was the case in Yokohama or Kobe. This also made visiting difficult, especially as transport facilities were now so crowded and inadequate. Kenneth confessed to getting very tired sometimes after a day of strap-hanging and of fighting his way on to trams and trains amid the blare of loud-speakers announcing destinations.

The Shingakuin carried on much as before, but faced considerable changes in the near future, for the Board of Education refused to allow any longer the existing relationship with Rikkyo. Instead the Shingakuin was to become a training school with a four year course instead of the existing three year course. This would be taken by non-graduates who would come direct from the high schools. Graduates of Rikkyo Religious Department would take only the last two years of the four year course. Kenneth felt this should be a great improvement and was one that he and others had been seeking over the last few years.

At the same time the college was faced with a serious decline in numbers. When Kenneth first started to teach there in 1934 each class had about twelve or fifteen students. Kenneth wrote in 1939 that the third year students were up to that number, but the second and first years were six and eight respectively. The following April four students were due to enter, the following year two from the University Junior Department, the following year none. Probably in each year there would be two or three non-graduate students as well, but the fact remained that the numbers were likely to decline from about forty to fewer than twenty. A big question would then arise in regard to the finances of the college, which were already none too secure, and in regard to the staff. Could a student body of fewer than twenty really require eight ordained men on the faculty?

From the time of his return to Japan from furlough, Kenneth greatly appreciated his role at the Embassy, which enabled him to keep in touch with political and military developments around the world. On 28 September 1938, just one month after that return, he wrote, "Well, things look about as black as they could be internationally and the odds seem pretty heavy on our being at war by the time this letter reaches you – if indeed it ever does."

A week later he wrote of the easing of tension following the Munich agreement, but added that he could not himself feel convinced about this 'new era of peace'. And indeed, within six months, Hitler proved how false his words were at Munich as German troops marched into Prague and took control of a Czechoslovakia left defenceless by the terms of that agreement. Now Chamberlain realised that Hitler would soon turn his attention to Poland and issued an undertaking that if any threat were offered to Poland then Britain would offer Poland all the support in its power.

Japan was cultivating friendly relations with Germany, while Britain was made the scapegoat for all Japan's misfortunes. Then towards the end of 1939 came the sudden announcement of the Soviet-German Non-Aggression Pact. Japan had looked upon Germany as an ally in opposing Soviet Russia. Now there was disgust at Germany's double-dealing.

That summer Kenneth and Ethelreda were staying in Takayama near Sendai with their children, but as the international situation grew ever more tense Kenneth returned to Tokyo, for only there could he hear the most up-to-date news. Each day he went to the Embassy and each day he wrote a letter to Ethelreda telling her of the unfolding situation. His last letter was sent on 3 September, reporting that Chamberlain had sent an ultimatum to Hitler requiring German acceptance of British demands for an immediate stop to the fighting in Poland and for a five-power conference, German acceptance to be into London before 12 noon (Tokyo 8 p.m.). When no such acceptance was received Britain declared war on Germany.

From the beginning of the War British residents were called to the Embassy for positive pep talks about the splendid progress of the allies and the certainty of a British victory. But then, in April, May, June 1940, came the 'blitzkrieg', Germany's lightning invasions of Denmark, Norway, Holland, Belgium and France, and it seemed that every time they emerged from these pep talks, the newsboys would be ringing their bells to announce that Hitler had overrun yet

**Kenneth as chaplain to the Royal Canadian
Air Force (RCAF)**

It would be eighteen years before Kenneth and Ethelreda returned to Japan. During the War Kenneth served as a chaplain in the Canadian Air Force and was posted to England, while his family remained in Canada. After the War he became Warden (Principal) of the Bishop's Hostel, a theological college in Lincoln, and then of St. Augustine's College, Canterbury, the Central College of the Anglican Communion.

In 1959 the NSKK celebrated the centenary of the arrival in Japan of the first Protestant missionaries. Archbishop Geoffrey Fisher arranged to make a tour through Asian countries, culminating in a visit to Japan to attend the celebrations. As Kenneth was also invited to Japan, the Archbishop suggested that he should accompany him as his chaplain. So, on 22 March, Archbishop and Mrs. Fisher, together with Kenneth and Ethelreda, set off on a 20,000 mile journey through Pakistan, India, Singapore, Hong Kong to Japan and Korea.

For the NSKK the destruction of war had been great, but now there were signs of recovery. Rikkyo had survived, but the Shingakuin had been destroyed by bombs, as had the house where Kenneth and his family had lived. Now the Shingakuin had resumed its work in new premises. In Shiba both the Japanese and the English St. Andrew's Churches had been burnt to the ground. Now a new St. Andrew's Church for Japanese congregations had been built and St. Alban's, a church for English-speaking, mainly American, congregations had been built. Bishop Yashiro, the Presiding Bishop of the NSKK, acknowledged the dark night through which both the Church and the Nation had travelled: "Now, as I stand with you all to celebrate this great occasion of the Centenary of the commencement of Protestant missionary work in this country, on this day of April 8, in the year 1959, I should like to say with you, 'Be thankful. Today I am still alive.'"

In 1961 Kenneth became the last English Bishop of Singapore and Malaya and from there was able to return again to Japan to meet friends and former students, many of them now in senior positions in the Church. In 1966 he returned to England to become General Secretary of the British Council of Churches before finally moving to Norwich in 1973.

Kenneth had gone to Japan as a young man in 1932 and might have expected to stay there for the rest of his career, but the War intervened and his life took a different course. Yet both Kenneth and Ethelreda retained a deep love of Japan. In his final report from Japan, written in 1940, Kenneth reflected on almost eight years spent in the country: "It has been a great privilege to serve in a land so beautiful, among a people so naturally kind and courteous...It is indeed a sad day for those who have admired Japan's fine achievements to see the disastrous course she is now following."

It was a great joy to both Kenneth and Ethelreda to return to Japan in 1959, to meet old friends and to see both the Church and the Nation on the way to recovery. Kenneth died in 1993 and Ethelreda in 1994.

ABOUT THE AUTHOR

Left to right: Ethelreda, Audrey (author),
Kenneth and Christopher (author's
brother)

ABOUT THE AUTHOR

44826142R00061

Printed in Poland
by Amazon Fulfillment
Poland Sp. z o.o., Wrocław